HANDWRITING ANALYSIS

AND

DETECTION OF DECEPTION

by

Larry M. McDaniel

ABOUT THE AUTHOR

Larry M. McDaniel was certified by the State of Georgia Merit System as Clinical Psychologist in 1976 and later as Senior Behavior Specialist in 1986. He has been engaged in the practice of handwriting analysis since that time period, also. He currently conducts psychological pre-employment screening and polygraph examinations for attorneys.

Mr. McDaniel began the study of handwriting analysis in the mid 1970's and began incorporating it into his pre-employment evaluations on a regular basis. He has done handwriting analysis for corporate placement and general screening for many years. He has become very interested in the use of handwriting analysis for detection of deception and is currently conducting on-going research in comparing handwriting analysis with polygraph results.

The author feels that more emphasis should be placed on the negative traits in handwriting analysis when a client's personal, financial or material interests are involved. He feels that handwriting analysis is one of the most valuable tools for employee

screening and placement that is available to us today.

INTRODUCTION

In my many years of work in criminal polygraph testing and general pre-employment screening, I have come to realize that there is a need for a format on handwriting analysis that emphasizes the negative traits rather than the positive.

When we are performing pre-employment screening for our clients, it behooves us to protect the client's assets from would-be-thieves, liars and downright criminals. The examples that you are about to study are true case histories that have been confirmed either by admissions, criminal background checks or polygraph examinations. These are people who are applying for jobs in positions of high financial and material responsibility. Some of the cases are from criminal investigations of theft, sexual crimes and other criminal activities.

When you see these traits in your applicant's sample be sure to give them ample consideration in your overall evaluation. Many analysts have never been around the criminal type and don't understand how the criminal mind works. They may have studied it in manuals or in come classroom cases; however, in a face-to-face situation it is very different. You don't want the criminal element as your client's employee.

INDEX

HANDWRITING ANALYSIS

AND

DETECTION OF DECEPTION

In Sample Number One, we are attempting to make a decision about hiring a man for a position as "parts man" for an automobile dealership. He will be responsible for many thousands of dollars in parts and inventory and will conduct parts sales over the counter and wholesale as well. It is a position that is vulnerable to theft and mismanagement.

Take a look at the sample and then make your determination as to whether or not you would recommend him for employment. Then, read the details on the following pages for the full story.

SAMPLE # 1

MOTIVATIONAL CONSIDERATION
Why do you want this job?   (Use cursive ONLY - DO NOT PRINT)

Signature

Date

The first thing that was observed was the extreme distortion in the date numbers at the lower left hand of the page. Anyone handling money should write with clear and distinct numbers. Overwriting and any type of distortion in numbers are indications of deception and concealment where money is concerned.

The next criteria that was noted was the extreme rightward slant in many of this applicant's letters. This indicates someone who is extremely impulsive and finds it difficult to control his or her impulses. When figures are distorted and the individual is impulsive, he already has two strikes against him.

An additional outstanding trait is the lower loop on the letter "f" strokes. They finish with a large hook going backward and to the left. In one study done some time ago in prisons, 80% of the convicted felons in the prison had this trait. Of course, one trait alone will not cause any type of problem or job rejection. However, when you combine the distorted numbers, extreme impulsiveness and the lower claw, his chances for getting recommended for the position are getting very slim, indeed.

The next trait that stuck out was the extreme backward slant to the lower loop on the "g" in "Volkswagen". This, coupled with the leftward claw on the "f" letters, give further indication of a troubled individual with extreme emotional impulsiveness and compulsion.

This individual confessed that he has stolen approximately $500.00 in miscellaneous parts and supplies from his former employer and to having used alcohol during working hours. He had also used marijuana during his teenage years along with speed, hashish and mushrooms until the age of 30. He is not 43 and drinks about four beers per day. He has a 10th grade education.

There are further indicators of this applicant's emotional disturbances. You can see double loops in the "a" and "o" letters. There are other factors involved but with so many already noted, it would not have been necessary to conduct any further analysis to determine this applicant's disposition.

In Sample Number Two, we have a young man applying for the position of porter at an automobile dealership. While not dealing with money, he will be in and out of both dealership vehicles as well as customer vehicles. He will have access to keys, parts and other merchandise of high value. His appearance was clean and neat and he had a very disarming smile and charm about him.

Make your evaluation based on the below sample and then compare your notes with the facts on the following pages.

SAMPLE NUMBER TWO

PORTER APPLICANT

MOTIVATIONAL CONSIDERATION

Why do you want this job? (Use cursive ONLY - DO NOT PRINT)

I want this job so that I can family and take care of me and I can better myself with this job up the letter.

(ENLARGED 22% FOR CLARIFICATION)

_____ ___ _ _____

Signature

5-29-92
Date

The first trait to get my attention was the left slant with the extreme leftward slanting "d". This indicates a self-interested regressive personality rather than an outward expressive personality. The next thing to get the eye is the extreme distortion in the father figure indicator in the personal pronoun "I". Notice how twisted the left lower portion of the personal pronoun "I" is all through his writing. This indicates much anger and/or conflict with some father figure in his early life.

You will further notice the distortions in the other letters such as the "s" in "so", the "o" in "of", the "a" in "and" and the "f" in "myself". Particularly look at the tick marks in the letter "c" of "care" and the additional stroke on the "t" in "letter" and overwrite on the "i" in "with" and in other letters. Overall, it could be easily seen that this young man had deep hostility going back into his past and, indeed, he was still living in the past with mental confusion and distortion of this thought processes clearly evident.

Upon conducting a criminal background investigation, it was discovered that this young man was a habitual offender and a drug dealer as well.

In Sample Number Three we have three hundred dollars missing from an office. The writing is from a secretary who had been working for several years at her place of employment and was a trusted employee.

See if you can discern the writing and make a determination if she had anything to do with the theft of the missing money.

SAMPLE NUMBER THREE

MISSING MONEY

The day started out pretty normal. Dana brought the deposit to the office and put it down on Rebecca's desk. Dee came in and said Mary could do the deposit today she then picked up the deposit and put it on Mary's desk. My sister and I were in the office My sister was in the file room at the time When Mary came in to do deposit she said there was only one envelope of cash on her desk they never found the other envelope

I did not steal the cash in the deposit.

In Sample Number Three we have a case of cash theft of $300.00 missing from a deposit in an office. The office manager was asked to write out what happened in longhand and was told that her last statement was to read that she did not steal that missing money and that she did not know who did steal the missing money.

The first thing that you will notice is the change in spacing on the fifth line from the top. When she states that she and her sister are in the room the line starts an upward climb. It returns to normal on the sixth line. You will also notice the distance between the next to the last line and the line in which she denied any involvement in the theft. This is an indication of trying to distance herself from the crime.

Her sister had, in fact, been in the room but had left for a brief period of time. It was during her sister's absence that she stole the money and that is why the line changes course when she lies in her description of events.

An additional factor is the curved live for the personal pronoun "I". Here we have an individual who likes to take the easy way out and doesn't make much effort in life. You will also notice the double loops on the "o" letters. Notice particularly, the distortion in the word "normal" on the first line and the distorted" on the fourth line from the top.

In discerning deception in a letter, look for distinct changes, overwrites, distortions or any other abnormality concerning the writer's description of the events leading up to the incident in question.

The lady in question proclaimed her innocence up to and through her interviews. However, when she failed the polygraph examination and was also confronted with the handwriting analysis conclusion she admitted the theft and agreed to make restitution to her employer.

In Sample Number Four you will find the writing of a man accused of stealing $1,000.00 from his employer's house. He was a personal friend of the employer and had house privileges for many months as he had been unemployed for some time until his friend hired him.

The employer had placed some cash in a drawer in his study and had taken his family on a short trip out of town. When he returned, he discovered that the money was missing and called the police. This sample was taken at the police department.

15

SAMPLE NUMBER FOUR

MISSING MONEY

When Me and   y   I
Was at   y fc House. I've been told
By the father that charles y left a pay
For   y. Me and   y returned
to that house on a thursday and
left me there untill Friday then He left again
to go away for two days We had and argu-
ment about the answering Machene. And he left me
sitting In his fathers car while he pulled away
In his own. With the thougt of either go
back to Augusta Ga or stay. His father called
and said stay. Which I did untill Saturday
night, I did not steal that Missing Money
          From Mr   Js Home

          Signed By

You will notice the rise in the word "money" on the last line and the overall drop in baseline of the entire sentence when he denies stealing the money. You will also notice the large number of "felon's claws" on the "y" and "g" letters. This person stole the money when his employer had left him alone in the house.

You will also notice the large indent on the last line. In both of the two last lines there is much deception shown. The spacing change, the "pop-up" word "money" on the end and the distancing of the lines from the other writing of the main statement.

He confessed and told everyone what he had done with money and where it could be found.

In Sample Number Five we are screening an applicant for the position of cashier. See what your think.

SAMPLE NUMBER FIVE

CASHIER APPLICANT

I want the position at and provide this company with my skills and abilities. Providing my skills + obtaining experience will give me the knowledge to prove to be an asset for the company.

This applicant was hired before she was screened. Shortly after her hiring the company came up with $526.00 missing from the cash drawer. Her sample came from her employee application form where she was asked to write out the reason why she wanted the job.

You will immediately notice the extreme distortions in the word "will" on the fourth line from the top. The downhill slant indicates a person with a depressed attitude. The left slant of the writing indicates someone who is into herself to the exclusion of others in her life. You will also notice the covered "a" letters and the loops in the "o" letters, indicating much deception and concealment.

In this example, the lady was a "thief of opportunity". She found money in the drawer that had not been properly entered in the records. She took the money and denied any knowledge of how it disappeared or who might have taken it. She failed the polygraph examination and subsequently confessed and repaid the money.

If the handwriting analysis had been done before she became a cashier, the company could have avoided the loss and saved much expense in recovering the loss and having to fire the thief.

In Samples Six and Seven on the next two pages we have samples of writing done by two jewelry store employees. There was $5,000.00 in cash missing. Did one of them do it? See what you think

SAMPLE NUMBER SIX

CASH THEFT

I noticed items missing right before inventory & I started looking for them on tape & then it was inventory & items were missing.

A few weeks later a school friend of a person that left the Co. on Fri before monday of inventory came in to ask about the same person - & to tell of an item missing from her house & told of a lot of Brac.'s the person had on. & two were on the missing list,

I have been with the Co - from July -   - til now I have never taking anything from the Co.

SAMPLE NUMBER SEVEN

CASH THEFT

I   started working for
October 16, 1991. In January after
inventory I became aware or was told that
several pieces of merchandise was missing
I didn't see any unusual things happen.
I didn't see anyone steal anything.
I will be willing to take a polygraph
test because I know I haven't taken
anything.
I have never stole anything from

3-31-92

In Sample Number Seven you can see some retracing of the "p", "n" and a few other letters. However, there are few deceptive traits. All lines are consistent with few distortions.

In Sample Number Six, however, you will notice a complete slant reversal, wide spacing in the lower portion of the letter and distortion in the word "never". when she denies any theft on her part. Also notice the stabbed oval in the word "from" on next to the last line. You will also notice the fluctuations in pressure during the last portion of the letter.

When confronted with the handwriting changes and other circumstances, she confessed to the theft and gave a written confession and agreement to make full restitution to her employer. She was the manager of the store and had been a trusted employee for many years. However, this lady had become romantically involved with a man who had a cocaine habit and she was financing his habit.

This case is of particular interest in that all five employees were given a polygraph examination and the examiner claimed that all had passed without any indication of deception on anyone's test.

However, you can easily see from the writing that the manager's writing shows clear evidence of deception. This is one case where were it not for handwriting analysis the thief would have gone free.

In Sample Number Eight we have a car sales applicant. See if you would put him in charge of your automobile inventory.

SAMPLE NUMBER EIGHT

CAR SALES

MOTIVATIONAL CONSIDERATION

Why do you want this job? (Use cursive ONLY - DO NOT PRINT)

I very much desire to be a productive member of my community again. I want to be self sufficient and not to depend upon anyone to take care of me. I desire to live within this society and abide by the laws. Although my past history may leave a lot of room for questions, I'm honestly asking for a chance to prove that I can function — as a law abiding citizen within my community

Signature

July 21st
Date

In Sample Number Eight you will notice on line one the angularity associated with the father figure in the personal pronoun "I". On line two you will notice the hooks on the lower loops of the "y" letters and the loops in the "o" and the "g" letters.

On line three notice the dashes for "i" dots rather than actual dots. This indicates anger and/or irritability. Notice the angularity of the "n" letters and the cover strokes of the "d" letters and the angle reaching back to the left on the down stroke of the "y" letters. The distortions continue on line six with more double loops in the "o" letters and angularity of the "y" and "m" letters, indicating much anger in this person. Particularly notice the large loop in the "o" in the word "honestly".

This applicant is a habitual liar with much hostility and anger. His writing pressure is heavy and if he becomes irritated by anyone he has no hesitation toward venting his anger in terms of doing harm to others.

The writer of Sample Number Eight served four years in prison for armed robbery, two years for robbery and kidnapping and a few years later was placed on probation for solicitation of prostitution. He was 42 and single at the time of this sample. He had used marijuana from his teenage years up to the present and cocaine as well.

In Sample Number Nine we see the writing of an applicant for the position of courier. What traits can you see that would help you render a decision on his recommendation for employment?

SAMPLE NUMBER NINE

COURIER APPLICANT

- -

MOTIVATIONAL CONSIDERATION

Why do you want this job? (Use cursive ONLY - DO NOT PRINT)

Is I cant have goals, be well off so I can to make it in the world. And to be a successful company.

In Sample Number Nine you will notice the filled in letters throughout the entire sample. There is a drop in the baseline and much twisted lettering throughout the sample. There is total confusion regarding this writer's identity that is summarized in the personal pronoun "I". The slant varies from left to right and the writing pressure is heavy.

Notice the flat upper zones indicating repression, the "tent" in the "t" letters indicating stubbornness, the extreme overwrites and many other traits indicating someone who is not to be trusted about anything,

This writer had been arrested and charged with child molestation. To employ such an applicant would have put the dealership in a precarious position and exposed them to serious potential damages in the future.

Even without the arrest report, this applicant would never have been recommended due to his totally deceptive personality. Again, handwriting analysis saved an employer from a potential disaster.

In Sample Number Ten an orderly is accused of assaulting a patient in a mental hospital. See if you think that he did it.

SAMPLE NUMBER TEN

PHYSICAL ASSAULT

ON December 8th I   WAS standing
in the Nurse's station talk with the Nurse
and a patient (A.Y.) That is when   got
out bed and started Across the unit to the bathroom,
Mr.   then took his penis out of his pants, that's
when I Aproached Mr.   down the. I Ask Mr.
to put his penis back in his pants Mr.   then
hit me in my mouth and grab my collar. I proceeded to
Restrain Mr.   by shoving him up against the wall
Mr.   immediatly turned my collar loose. I proceded
to restrain Mr.   by turning him around and grabbin
his collar from behind. I took the patient Mr.
down the hall and thru the unit and him in time-a
I then informed the Nurse what had ocurred. I
            Knowingly Injure Mr.   Danny

Danny
1-4-93

The orderly was asked to write in cursive (not print) an account of what happened and to deny that he had deliberately hit the patient. After he wrote the account he was put on the polygraph for an examination.

The subject did refuse to cooperate at first but when it was explained that he was under suspicion for felony assault and could be charged unless he could verify his innocence he then consented for the polygraph and anything else that was asked of him.

This person could write in cursive but chose to write in script. This was the first red flag. This indicates an attempt to conceal information and shows probable deception to start with. You will also notice the many heavy overwrites on many of the letters. The overall pressure of the writing was heavy with frequent intense pressure. This shows volatility and explosiveness.

One of the most noticeable signs of guilt in the handwriting was the writer's total omission of the words "I did not" on the last line when he was supposedly denying deliberate injury to the patient. As a matter of fact, he left the space blank where the writing was supposed to be.

The subject did fail the polygraph examination and, later, two witnesses came forth and stated that they had seen him beating the patient.

Did the writer in Sample Number Eleven have inappropriate sexual contact with a 13 year old girl? Make your determination and then compare your results with those on the following page.

SAMPLE NUMBER ELEVEN

STATUTORY RAPE

The Night of 18 Aug.
we were watching TV me And the three girls
we were watch the Braves BlAying Bal
The Girls mother Had to go to Work.
She told them They HAd to go To Bed At 11
They wanting ToStAy up Awhile
I Let Them STAy up tell 11:15 To 11:3o
The Girls went To Bed I SeT And wAtch
The Rest of The BAll SAme.   An
got BAck up They went to The Frig. got
wine They Ask me if they eould Drink iT
I Told them no But They Drink it
me And The Two Girl BIAy cards
Drink A little   Drink most of
The wine wAJ gone They went To Bed
got BAck up 2 times
I mAde Her go BACK To Bed I Told Her J
Could Not STAy in There with me.

This is another example of the subject being instructed to write in cursive but wrote in print form instead. Notice the filled in letters, (pastiosity), overwrites, retracing and heavy pressure. All of this indicates a writer with extreme sensitivity to sexual urges and an inability to control them.

You will also notice that the line spacing gets very erratic toward the middle of the letter and the base line starts to go up and down much more than at any other time. The more he lies, the greater is the variance of the writing as he goes along.

This writer was 38 at the time of the sample. He had been drinking beer while watching TV with two teenage girls. The girls started drinking wine and one drank an entire bottle of wine. She admitted to having instigated the sexual incident. All of this was written in her diary.

When the girl's father discovered the information in his daughter's diary, he immediately filed charges against the subject. The subject failed the polygraph examination and subsequently confessed.

In Sample Number Twelve a man is accused of molesting his granddaughter. See what you think.

SAMPLE NUMBER TWELVE

CHILD MOLESTATION

I got out of   town Detention Center on aug 2 4
and spent 7 or 8 Day's at Mrs   or behind her
house in a Camper and the first 3 or 4 Day's
I spent around 1 hour a day with My granddaughter playing in the front yard except on
one time with me and my wife cooked out back
and I was left alone with her the granddaughter
for about 15 or 20 minutes on sept 21 she was
taken to the Doc. by my wife and they said
she had been moolested and I was arrested
the following day

I did not Molest L 1   in any way
nor do I Know who did

In Sample Number Twelve the writer is accused of molesting his granddaughter. He was given instructions to hand write a description of events leading up to his arrest and to write that he had not done what he was accused of. It was explained to him that this was his "statement of innocence".

When he finished the statement he had totally "forgotten" to make the statement of innocence. His omission was the first indication that he may be guilty. When he did write his innocence statement, you will notice that he baseline of the writing slanted noticeably downhill.

Upon reading the document you will notice that the time he mentions of "20 minutes" is elevated. This indicates that something took place during this period of time that excited him in some way and he doesn't want to divulge it. Since he was writing about molesting his granddaughter it was another indication of probably guilt.

On the third line from the bottom you will notice the extremely left leaning lower loops on the words "following day". When the lower loops lean far to the left and in excess of the average slant of the letters it is usually indicative of sexual attachment to the past and/or sexual maladjustment and also early childhood sexual fixations.

The writer failed his polygraph examination. Also, the police were given a statement from the child and other circumstantial evidence. He then confessed in writing and made a full account of the actual incident.

In Sample number Thirteen we have another child molestation case.

This writer wasn't well educated enough to write in cursive so his print script wasn't an indication of deception in and of itself. The circumstances were that he and a preteen girl were in the house of his girl friend while she was out. He had been drinking beer all day long and he bragged that he had drunk 32 beers that day.

Make an analysis on this writer and compare your notes to those on the page following the sample.

CHILD MOLESTATION

I got up around 9:00 am. 12-7-92. I called (STEPFATHER) He
wanted me to come up and check The anitfreeze in His son's
motorcycle, I we their, we got drunk, (GRANDFATHER) waz
their, ~~████████████~~ wanted me to take
to the store. started saying that He would that me?
mite do (something sexual) so I cussed Him out and He went
to the store And came back. every thing was okay so we drank
some more. me and. Road around and dronk more
beer. It was about 10:00 o'clock my wife came up And
waz gripping because I wasn't at Home she went out to the
car To get my key's seen beer waz poured all in it, she came
back in And we got into a big fuss. She grabed my coat
And Left! I was thlking on the telephone when she left. I got
off the phone and was wathing a footBall game w/.
Till passed out. I thing everyone just went to Bed Because, told
me to set up she had fixxed me a palet in the loundey Room
I went And Layed Down And got woke up By Fussing
at angle, wanting to know what she was doing in their, I don't know
whare waz standing, sixing, Laying All I know She
were at my feet. I was Tired of Fussing so I walked up
To my mother's About 200 yds away
I didn't Touch. Brest or
Virgina!

12-21-93

Notice the ink filled letters (pastiosity) in this writing. Also notice the rapid upswing of the misspelled word "brest or" on the last line.

Without any other evidence or any polygraph examination the handwriting analyst leans to probable guilt in this case. He was subsequently polygraphed and did confess and gave a written statement concerning the entire situation.

In Sample Number Fourteen and fifteen we get a chance to see a "before and after" situation. The writer was interviewed concerning working at a jewelry store. Her answers to the psychological evaluation were satisfactory and her personal interview went will with the Human Resources person in charge of hiring at the store. She had indicated some personal problems in the past but nothing that would preclude her getting the job. Also, she had prior sales experience in the jewelry business.

After working for a few weeks $2,000.00 came up missing. Since there were about six employees that had access to the money she wasn't singled out but included in the overall investigation.

Take a look and see if you can any differences in the "before" employment and "after" starting to work there.

SAMPLE NUMBER FOURTEEN AND FIFTEEN

CASH THEFT

MOTIVATIONAL CONSIDERATION

Why do you want this job? (Use cursive ONLY - DO NOT PRINT)

The last job I had in sales was the most enjoyable work that I have ever done, I use to really look forward to going to work with that company, I want the sales position job at _____ because I see alot of growth potential with this company. I will be getting a lot more than a paycheck, my goals and growth with the company will totally depend on me. I really enjoy working with the public and I have great public relation skills.

Signature

7·6·93

I took one jumpring to repair an earring.

I have worked since July of 1993, my duties are to come in as schedule and do my daily task as planed for the day. Number one being selling.

I have not stolen money or merchandise from

After working for the jewelry store, this writer became involved in a relationship with a drug dealer. There were indications that this was an earlier relationship and that she had gotten back together with this person. She got into cocaine and alcohol and did steal the missing $2,000.00 from her employer.

Notice the change in writing. You can see the tremors in the writing in the bottom sample (Sample Number Fifteen) along with the twists of the lower loops and the downward slant. The spacing is greater between the lines in the lower sample and what you will notice most of all is her great gap between the main body of the writing and her denial of any theft from her employer.

The other employees had noticed mood swings, behavioral changes and an inability to do what she was told or to learn new procedures.

Take a look at Sample Number Sixteen and see if you would hire this person to work for you.

SAMPLE NUMBER SIXTEEN

CASHIER APPLICANT

Because the Location is very conjeneaht to me and has atmosphere for working.

This applicant was applying for the position of cashier at a gas station. He tested positive on cocaine on the day he wrote the above sample.

He admitted to having used marijuana from the age of 15 until 26. He had used crack cocaine from the age of 30 to 31. He was arrested recently for DUI and possession of cocaine.

As you examine the sample you will note the distortion in some of the letters. Note the "o" in "location", the "o" in

"Convenient" (He misspelled the word in the sample), the "o" in "to", the "s" in "atmosphere" and the "o" in "or".

A further analysis shows a high degree of variability in the "e" in "because" compared with other "e" letters in the writing. Also, note the cover strokes in the "c" in "because", the disconnected letters in the words, the unusual "i" dot in "location" and the added strokes on the word "to" and "for". You will also note the retracing and add-on lettering.

Even without drug screening, this applicant should not be placed with any client you may have and should not be recommended for any position of employment with anyone you are hired to protect.

Take a look at the writing in Sample Number Seventeen and see if you would recommend him.

SAMPLE NUMBER SEVENTEEN

, Because i need this Job. Because im getting
Behind in my bills and d. know everyone
thats works there and d will make a good
) Employee to Jax.

In Sample Number Seventeen you will notice many "ticks" in this writer's hand. Ticks usually always indicate drug use. It is an interference of the writer's thought process and it is reflected in aberrations in his script.

Take a look at Sample Number Eighteen and see if you can see the drug use.

SAMPLE NUMBER EIGHTEEN

Signature

The above writer in Sample Number Eighteen tested positive for cocaine and marijuana at the time of this writing. Notice the variable slant and the variation in word size and style change from thread writing to slower writing. There are many other factors to study here that reveal a totally unacceptable applicant for employment.

Take a look at Sample Number nineteen. Here you will see an applicant that was on amphetamines and marijuana at the time of the writing.

SAMPLE NUMBER NINETEEN

- -
MOTIVATIONAL CONSIDERATION
Why do you want this job? (Use cursive ONLY - DO NOT PRINT)

Personal friends with Bob + I know its a good company.

_____
Signature

3-3-93
Date

PARAMETERS OF DECEPTION

When making an assessment of truthfulness, there are many traits to compare. The below list is only a representative segment of the numerous signs that you can discern for deception.

HONESTY	DECEPTION
Even baseline	Uneven Baseline
Firm pressure	Light/variable pressure
Right slant tendency	Left slant tendency
Legibility	Illegibility
Free movement	Cramped, retraced, slow
Short initials	Initial hooks, claws
Even midzone heights	Uneven midzone - jump up letters
Copybook capital I	Extremes in capital I
Consistency	Inconsistency
Ovals clear	Ovals embellished, looped on left or right, double loops at bottom
Script easy to read	Scrip difficult to read
Clear letters	Coiled letters

Consistent slant	Changing slant
Straight lines	Jumbled but legible
Finished strokes	Unfinished strokes or letters
Full script	Thread-like script
No arcades	Arcades in letters or script
No cover strokes	Covered strokes
No flourishes	Flourished letters
Even words or strokes	Tapered words or strokes
Same size of letters	Varying size of letters
Capital letters on baseline	Improvements or corrections in words already written
Same writing	Several different writings
Capital letters on baseline	Capital letters below baseline
End strokes do not plunge	End strokes plunge into lower zone.
Clear script	Superfluous or heavy dots in script
Same signature and writing	Very different signature from writing
Regular spacing and pressure	Odd, irregular spacing and pressure
Regular writing speed	Irregular writing speed
"a" and "o" closed	"a" and "o" open at bottom with clockwise strokes
Normal size "I"	Oversize "I"

COMMENTS

When making an honesty evaluation it is necessary to note that one or two traits do not indicate that your subject is dishonest. However, five or more traits in one given sample of writing is a good indication of dishonesty and deception.

You have to be able to determine to what degree the writing leans from honesty to dishonesty and to make a fair balance in assessing your applicant's job duties and your client's best interest. Obviously, you want to protect your client's interests and will therefore screen out applicants who have an excessive number of deceptive traits.

www.ingramcontent.com/pod-product-compliance
Lightning Source LLC
Chambersburg PA
CBHW061230280526
45784CB00006B/2709